BEAUTY AND THE BEAST

AND OTHER FAIRY TALES

ILLUSTRATED BY RENE CLOKE

GALLERY BOOKS
An Imprint of W. H. Smith Publishers Inc.

BEAUTY SAW THE PRINCE OF HER DREAMS

CONTENTS

BEAUTY AND THE BEAST

ONE day a rich merchant set off on a journey, promising to bring each of his three daughters a present. The two eldest were greedy and asked for jewels and fine clothes. But Beauty only asked for one small thing – a red rose.

Unluckily, the merchant lost all his goods and money. On his way home he came to a fine palace. Inside were a welcoming fire, food and a warm bed – but no people. The merchant was so tired and hungry he went inside, had dinner and went to bed. Next morning he was about to leave when he saw a fine rose bush. Remembering Beauty, he picked one perfect red rose for her.

HE PICKED A ROSE FOR HIS DAUGHTER

Immediately, the merchant heard a huge roar. To his horror, a terrible Beast appeared, screaming, "You shall die for this, you ungrateful man! Food and warmth you are welcome to, but nobody is allowed to touch my precious roses!"

The poor merchant pleaded with the Beast, "Forgive me, please. I only wanted one bloom for my very special daughter, Beauty."

"I will spare your life on one condition," the Beast said. "You must send your daughter to me in return."

Sadly the merchant returned home and told Beauty what the Beast had said. He did not want her to go, but Beauty said, "I am not afraid. I am only grateful you are safe. We must keep the promise."

When Beauty reached the palace and saw the Beast, she felt very frightened.

"Good day, Sir," she whispered, with a curtsy. "I have come to thank you for the rose, and for giving my father shelter and sparing his life."

"Your father is a lucky man to have such a beautiful daughter," said the

BEAUTY CURTSIED TO THE BEAST

Beast in a voice that was not unkind.

"He is not such a terrible Beast after all," thought Beauty, smiling timidly.

"Stay and keep me company for a while," the Beast asked. Beauty felt sorry for him, so for a whole month she stayed as a guest. Every day Beauty and the Beast walked together in the palace gardens, and in the evening she sang for him. Each day, she grew less afraid of the Beast and even looked forward to being with him. But at night she always had the same mysterious dream. She dreamed she was walking in the gardens with a handsome Prince. As time went by she realized she had fallen in love with the Prince in her dreams.

Beauty would sit by the pool in the palace gardens for hours, thinking only of her dreams, until the Beast came to join her for their walk among the flowers.

Only one thing troubled her. Every evening before they parted, the Beast asked Beauty the same two questions.

SHE SAT BY THE POOL AND DREAMED

"Do you really think I am ugly?" he would ask her first.

And being a very truthful girl, Beauty had to say that she did. "But I know you are the kindest, gentlest Beast there ever was," she added.

Then the Beast would ask the second question. "Will you marry me?"

"No, I cannot do that," said Beauty, "for I do not love you enough."

"Do you love someone else then?" the Beast wanted to know.

"Yes," Beauty would whisper, thinking of the Prince in her dreams.

So every night the Beast went away, looking very sad.

After a time, Beauty began to feel very sad too. She was homesick and missed her father. She even missed the loud chattering and quarrelsome company of

THE QUESTIONS WERE ALWAYS THE SAME

her two bad-tempered sisters with their constant demands.

One night she dreamed that her father was ill and was calling for her. Next morning she told the Beast about her dream and begged him to let her go home for a visit.

"You are such a good, kind girl that I must let you go to him and help him get well," the Beast agreed. "But promise to return to me in one month, or I shall die of a broken heart," he added.

"I shall miss you, Beast, you are so kind and good to me," Beauty said. Then she gave him her promise. But she was so excited at the thought of going home that she forgot it almost immediately.

The Beast sent Beauty home in a fine carriage, which made her sisters more jealous than ever. But Beauty was too happy to notice, and her father began to feel better the moment he saw her.

A month passed very quickly at home. Beauty nursed her father until he was completely better. At the same time she

HER FATHER WAS GLAD TO SEE HER

had to keep the peace between her two sisters, who argued and fought a great deal. They disliked Beauty but found it very useful to have her back at home. Every time she suggested leaving them to return to the Beast as she had promised, they found another excuse for her to stay with them.

Soon, another month had passed and still Beauty was at home. She no longer had any dreams about the Prince, but one night she found herself dreaming about the Beast's palace garden. In her dream, she seemed to be walking among a tangle of roses. From somewhere nearby she could hear terrible moans and groans.

"Someone needs help," she thought. Then in her dream she came upon the Beast, lying on the ground weeping. He

seemed terribly ill and broken-hearted.
Suddenly Beauty remembered the
promise she had made to return within
a month and awoke with a cry of despair. How could she break a promise to

THE BEAST LOOKED AS IF HE WAS DYING

anyone who had treated her so well?

The next morning, she told her father and her sisters that she wanted to return to the Beast's palace immediately. Of course they tried to persuade her to stay. Her father was afraid to lose his dearest daughter again, and her selfish sisters dreaded having to do all the work Beauty had done. But she was determined to go, and so they had to let her.

As soon as she reached the palace, Beauty rushed into the gardens. Sure enough, the place had become a tangle of roses. She found the Beast, lying sick and weeping, just as in her dream.

"Please don't die, Beast," she said, touching him gently. "I have come back to help you."

At the sound of her voice he sat up.

"Oh, Beauty, why did you leave me

for so long? I cannot live without you!"
he said. Beauty threw her arms around
his rough neck, saying, "I love you,

HE SAT UP WHEN SHE TOUCHED HIM

Beast. What can I do to make you better?" She realized, at last, that she really did love him, so she gave him a kiss.

"Will you marry me, Beauty?" he asked her once more.

"Yes, dear Beast, I will," she said. Suddenly, everything changed. The Beast seemed to vanish, and there in front of her stood the Prince she had seen so often in her dreams.

"Thank you, Beauty, your true love has broken the spell put on me by a wicked fairy," the Prince said to her in the Beast's familiar voice.

So the pair were married and lived happily ever after.

THERE STOOD THE PRINCE

ALADDIN AND HIS MAGIC LAMP

LONG ago, in far-off China, lived a boy called Aladdin. He was the only son of a poor washerwoman, and his father had been dead for many years. Aladdin was a lazy boy. Instead of helping his mother, he just sat in the sun.

One day a stranger visited the house. "I am your long-lost Uncle Ebenezer," the man told Aladdin. "I could do with a strong young lad to help me with my work. How would you like to earn a purseful of gold in one day?" he asked.

Aladdin liked the idea of getting rich

quickly, so he agreed to lend a hand.

"What must I do?" he asked, hoping the work would not involve too much effort, for he was a very lazy boy.

"DO YOU WANT TO EARN SOME MONEY?"

"Just follow me, my boy," said the old man. At the edge of the town he stopped. At his feet was an iron ring fixed to a rock. He pulled on it, lifting up a trapdoor. Below were some steps leading down into a cave. Aladdin could see something shining like gold!

"Take this purse, my boy. Fill it up for yourself. And here is a ring to protect you. All I want you to do is bring me an old lamp that is lying in the corner," his uncle said.

Aladdin climbed through the trapdoor and went down the steps. He could hardly believe his eyes. There were heaps of money and jewels of every shape and size all around the cave.

"Hurry up, boy! I hear someone coming," his uncle called. "Bring me the lamp."

"JUST BRING UP THE OLD LAMP"

Aladdin filled his pockets with jewels, and he had just picked up the lamp when the trapdoor shut with a crash. He began to feel cold and frightened. Rubbing his hands to warm them, he felt his uncle's ring. Suddenly, there was a terrific flash, and a huge figure appeared.

"Who are you?" Aladdin cried out.

"I am the Genie of the Ring," said the figure. "If ever you are in danger, rub the ring and I will always rescue you."

"Take me home, then," pleaded Aladdin – and in an instant he was home. He showed his mother the jewels and money, and she tried to polish the lamp. As soon as she rubbed it, another Genie appeared, saying, "I am the Genie of the Lamp. What is your command?"

Aladdin's mother nearly fainted in surprise at the amazing sight. First the

A GENIE APPEARED IN A FLASH

jewels, and now magic spirits! But then Aladdin explained the whole story and made her promise to keep it a secret.

They soon put the lamp to good use and ordered the Genie to bring rich food, fine clothes, money and jewels. Whenever they needed more, they just gave the lamp a rub and the Genie appeared.

A few years later Aladdin had become so rich and famous that he asked for the hand of the Emperor's daughter in marriage. He gave the Emperor many splendid gifts and built a beautiful new palace opposite the Emperor's own. The news of Aladdin's marriage to the Princess reached the ears of his Uncle Ebenezer.

"That wretched boy must have escaped with the magic lamp!" he said angrily. "But I know how I can get it back."

Aladdin's uncle disguised himself as someone selling lamps.

"New lamps for old!" he called as he

wandered through the streets. People were glad to exchange their empty old lamps for new ones full with oil.

At last he reached Aladdin's palace and stood right under the Princess's window calling, "New lamps for old!"

"Why don't I buy Aladdin a new lamp?" thought the Princess. "That old one he keeps in our room is a disgrace. Everything else in the palace is new and sparkling, but I can never persuade him to throw it away, or even to let me ask a servant to polish it." For Aladdin had never told her its secret – which is just what the wicked uncle had guessed.

As soon as he got his hands on the lamp the wicked old man rubbed it and commanded the Genie to carry him away, along with the palace and the Princess.

The Emperor was furious with Aladdin and threw him into prison.

Sitting in his dungeon cell, Aladdin rubbed his hands in despair. But he had forgotten that he was still wearing the magic ring. The Genie of the Ring

appeared in a puff of smoke.

When Aladdin saw the Genie, he commanded, "Save me and bring my palace and the Princess back."

"Only the Genie of the Lamp can do that," answered the Genie of the Ring.

"Then take me to the Princess," Aladdin cried. Instantly, he was by her side. Aladdin snatched the lamp from his astonished uncle and rubbed it, and the Genie appeared.

"Take us back to China with the palace," Aladdin ordered, while the bewildered Princess clung to him in terror.

Uncle Ebenezer was so frightened by Aladdin's rapid appearance that he turned tail and ran. He was never seen or heard of again. Aladdin and his Princess were so happy to be together once more.

The palace flew through the air, taking them with it. The Emperor was so delighted at his daughter's safe return that he gave them all his kingdom.

THE PALACE FLEW THROUGH THE AIR

HANSEL AND GRETEL

HANSEL and Gretel were two children who had a kind father but a cruel, greedy stepmother. One night Hansel heard his stepmother say, "There just isn't enough food to feed all four of us. The children will have to go and find food for themselves in the woods."

After hearing this, Hansel crept downstairs and filled his pockets with small white pebbles from the garden.

The next day the children were taken to help fetch wood from the forest.

As they walked along, Hansel dropped

the pebbles out of his pocket, a few at a
time. They shone like stars on the path.
It began to get dark, and the children

HANSEL KEPT DROPPING PEBBLES

got lost. But by following Hansel's trail of shining pebbles, they found their way back home.

Their father was very glad to see them safely back, but their stepmother was not at all pleased. That night she locked all the doors so that Hansel could not get out to collect any pebbles.

When the children were sent back to the woods the next morning, all Hansel had in his pocket was a dry crust of bread.

Hansel began scattering crumbs along

the path. To begin with, they looked like tiny stones. But the birds flew down and ate them all. When, once again, the children found they were lost, they looked for the trail to lead them home. But there were no crumbs left. In the darkness they could not find the path.

In the forest Hansel and Gretel slept a

THE BIRDS ATE UP ALL THE CRUMBS

little. Then they wandered on until they came to a clearing where a pretty little house stood. They ran up to the door.

"What a beautiful house," said Gretel.

"It looks as if it is made of gingerbread and candy. Let's taste a bit."

She broke a piece off the window and nibbled it. "It's made of barley sugar!" she cried with delight.

Hansel began to eat some gingerbread. They were both very hungry.

"Who's that nibbling at my window?" cried a cracked voice from inside, and out hobbled an old witch. "Oh, it's two little children, is it?" she cackled when she saw Hansel and Gretel. "Come inside and do as I tell you," she said.

As soon as the door was shut, the old witch grabbed Hansel. Before Gretel could stop her, she had pushed him into

THE HOUSE WAS MADE OF GINGERBREAD

a huge cage and locked the door.

Gretel was given all the housework to do, but all the time she watched for a chance to rescue Hansel.

Each morning the witch went up to the cage to see how Hansel looked. He was given enormous meals to fatten him up, while poor Gretel had hardly any food.

"Show me your finger," the witch would demand, and Hansel was supposed to push out a finger for her to test its plumpness. But because she could not see well, Hansel would stick an old chicken bone through the bars. "Still just skin and bone. Not ready yet," she would mutter.

At last the witch could not wait any longer. "Light the oven, Gretel," she ordered.

Gretel lit the fire under the big oven. "Is the oven hot enough yet?" the witch asked Gretel.

"I do not know," said Gretel. "How can I find out? Will you show me?"

"It's simple, girl," grumbled the witch. "Just open the oven door like this and then put your head in, like this . . . " But she never said another word. For, quick as a flash, Gretel shoved the wicked witch into the oven and shut the door. And that was the end of her.

The spell on the little house was broken. A fawn the witch had captured showed Hansel and Gretel the way home. They took the witch's gold with them. When they got home, their father was delighted to see them.

He told them their stepmother had died. At last they were rich, and the three of them lived happily together again.

A LITTLE FAWN SHOWED THEM THE WAY